# COOL CASTLES AND PALACES
# DRACULA'S CASTLE

by Clara Bennington

pogo

# Ideas for Parents and Teachers

Pogo Books let children practice reading informational text while introducing them to nonfiction features such as headings, labels, sidebars, maps, and diagrams, as well as a table of contents, glossary, and index.

Carefully leveled text with a strong photo match offers early fluent readers the support they need to succeed.

## Before Reading

- "Walk" through the book and point out the various nonfiction features. Ask the student what purpose each feature serves.
- Look at the glossary together. Read and discuss the words.

## Read the Book

- Have the child read the book independently.
- Invite him or her to list questions that arise from reading.

## After Reading

- Discuss the child's questions. Talk about how he or she might find answers to those questions.
- Prompt the child to think more. Ask: What did you know about Bran Castle before you read this book? What else would you like to learn?

Pogo Books are published by Jump!
5357 Penn Avenue South
Minneapolis, MN 55419
www.jumplibrary.com

Library of Congress Cataloging-in-Publication Data

Names: Bennington, Clara, author.
Title: Dracula's castle / by Clara Bennington.
Description: Minneapolis, MN: Pogo Books are published by Jump!, Inc., 2020.
Series: Cool castles and palaces
Includes index. | Audience: Age 7-10.
Identifiers: LCCN 2018059358 (print)
LCCN 2019000022 (ebook)
ISBN 9781641288620 (ebook)
ISBN 9781641288613 (hardcover : alk. paper)
Subjects: LCSH: Castelul Bran (Bran, Brasov, Romania)
Juvenile literature. | Vlad III, Prince of Wallachia,
1430 or 1431-1476 or 1477--Juvenile literature.
Dracula, Count (Fictitious character) –Juvenile literature.
Classification: LCC DR240.5.V553 (ebook)
LCC DR240.5.V553 B46 2020 (print) | DDC 949.8/4–dc23
LC record available at https://lccn.loc.gov/2018059358

Editor: Jenna Trnka
Designer: Molly Ballanger

Photo Credits: warmcolors/iStock, cover; Wojciech Tchorzewski/Shutterstock, 1; Dmitriy Feldman svarshik/Shutterstock, 3, 23; Janos Gaspa/Dreamstime, 4; Trifuion/Dreamstime, 5; Aleksandar Todorovic/Shutterstock, 6-7; Anton_Ivanov, 8; Fotokon/Shutterstock, 9; Balate Dorin/Shutterstock, 10-11; Illustrated London News Ltd/Pantheon/SuperStock, 12; Dziewul/Dreamstime, 13; trabantos/Shutterstock, 14-15; CCat82/Shutterstock, 16-17, 20-21; Ryzhkov Sergey/Shutterstock, 18-19.

Printed in the United States of America at Corporate Graphics in North Mankato, Minnesota.

# TABLE OF CONTENTS

# CHAPTER 1

## COUNT DRACULA'S CASTLE

Perched on a cliff near Transylvania sits a castle. Count Dracula waits inside for the sun to set. Why? So he can satisfy his thirst for blood. Scary!

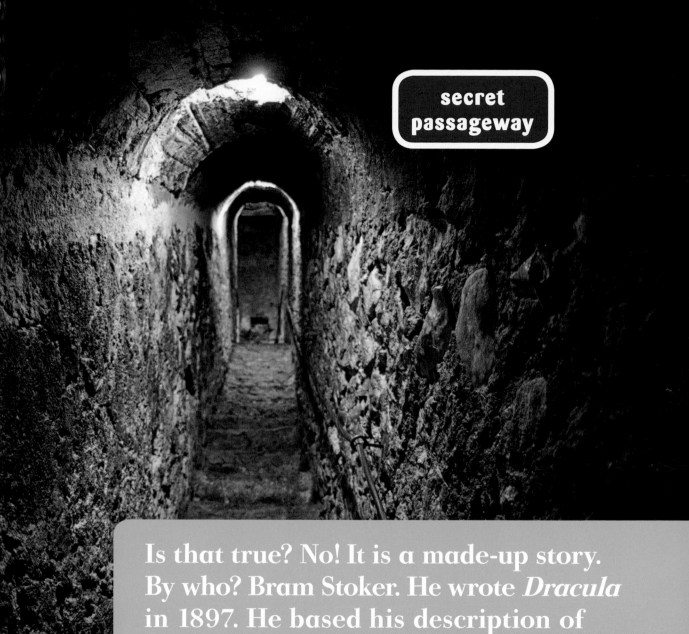

secret
passageway

Is that true? No! It is a made-up story.
By who? Bram Stoker. He wrote *Dracula*
in 1897. He based his description of
Dracula's home on Bran Castle. It is
a castle in Bran, Romania. It is filled
with secret passageways!

turret

In 1377, King Louis I of Hungary wanted to **defend** the **border** from **invaders**. He ordered villagers to clear the woods. He also ordered them to supply wood and stones. They would build him a beautiful castle. Look at the high **turrets**!

**DID YOU KNOW?**

In 1459, Vlad the Impaler attacked people in Romania. He **impaled** his enemies. He may have been the **inspiration** for Dracula!

# CHAPTER 2

# WAR AND DAMAGE

Soldiers lived in the castle. Weapons helped them protect it and the **goods** inside. The castle held goods moving in and out of nearby towns.

COURAGE

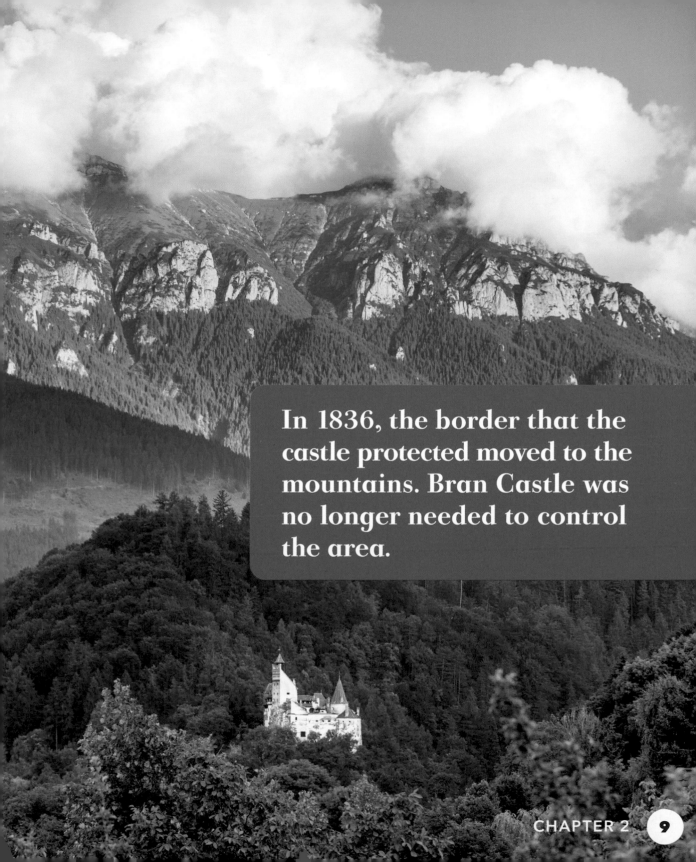

In 1836, the border that the castle protected moved to the mountains. Bran Castle was no longer needed to control the area.

The castle was damaged in the Romanian Revolution (1848). It was damaged again during the Russian-Turkish War (1877–1878). **Citizens** wanted the castle repaired. Work was done between 1883 and 1886.

## WHAT DO YOU THINK?

From 1888 to 1918, the castle fell back into disrepair. Foresters and woodsmen lived in it. Do you think it would have been fun to live in the castle?

# CHAPTER 3

# HOME FOR ROYALTY

In 1920, citizens in the area voted. The castle would go to Romania's Queen Marie. She wanted to use it as a summer home.

Queen Marie

Queen Marie had the castle fixed. She added a park and two ponds. She turned the well into an elevator. Why? It helped her get to the park faster.

well

tea house

She also added a tea house. It is now open to the public! Enjoy tea on the grounds.

## WHAT DO YOU THINK?

Queen Marie had a **power plant** built. It provided **electricity** to the castle and three nearby towns! How do you think this made the citizens feels about the **royal** family?

She wanted to keep the castle's **style**. The doors are low. People have to duck! She kept the heavy beams across the ceilings, too. The music room is the largest room in the castle.

music room

dining hall

Queen Marie added a hunting house and a **chapel**. She added stables and a garage. She also had a house built for her daughter, Princess Ileana. The dining hall is where the queen hosted guests.

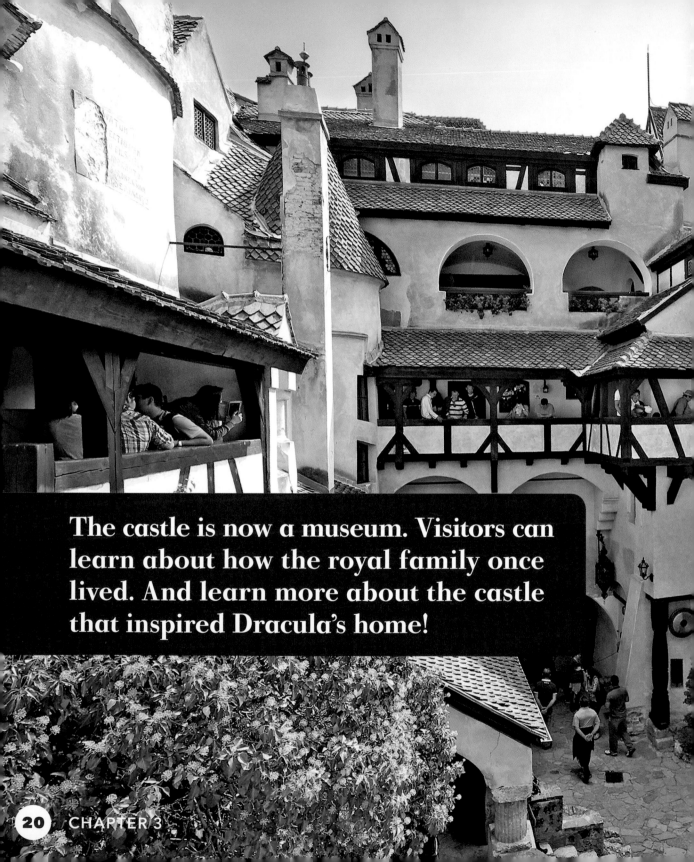

The castle is now a museum. Visitors can learn about how the royal family once lived. And learn more about the castle that inspired Dracula's home!

# TAKE A LOOK!

There are three main castle types. Bran Castle is considered a stone keep. What makes these castles different?

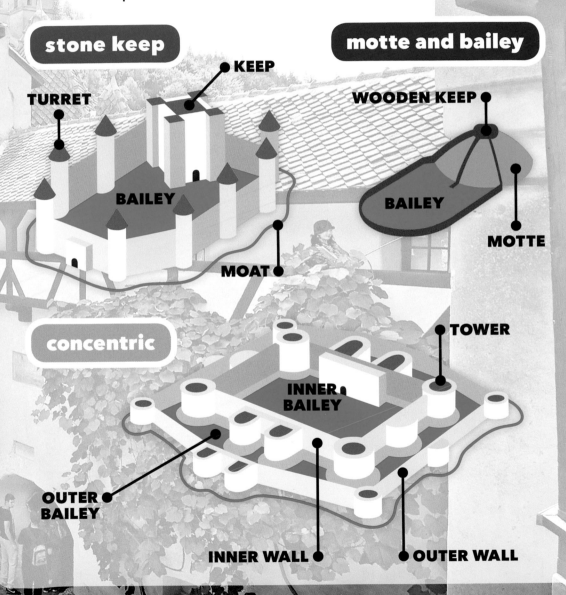

**stone keep**

KEEP

TURRET

BAILEY

MOAT

**motte and bailey**

WOODEN KEEP

BAILEY

MOTTE

**concentric**

TOWER

INNER BAILEY

OUTER BAILEY

INNER WALL

OUTER WALL

# QUICK FACTS & TOOLS

## AT A GLANCE

## BRAN CASTLE

**Location:** Bran, Romania

**Year Construction Began:** 1377

**Size (including grounds):**
787 acres (318 hectares)

**Number of Rooms:** 57

**Current Use:** Museum

**Average Number of Visitors
Each Year:** 835,000

# GLOSSARY

**border:** The dividing line between two countries or regions.

**chapel:** A small church.

**citizens:** Residents of a particular town or city.

**defend:** To protect from harm.

**electricity:** Power that is generated in plants and distributed through wires.

**goods:** Things that are sold.

**impaled:** Pierced with something pointed.

**inspiration:** Something that gives someone an emotion, an idea, or an attitude.

**invaders:** People who enter an area for conquest or plunder.

**power plant:** A building that generates electric power.

**royal:** Related to a king or queen or a member of his or her family.

**style:** The way in which something looks.

**turrets:** Round or square towers on a building.

# INDEX

# TO LEARN MORE

Finding more information is as easy as 1, 2, 3.

1 Go to www.factsurfer.com

2 Enter "Dracula'sCastle" into the search box.

3 Choose your book to see a list of websites.

FACT SURFER